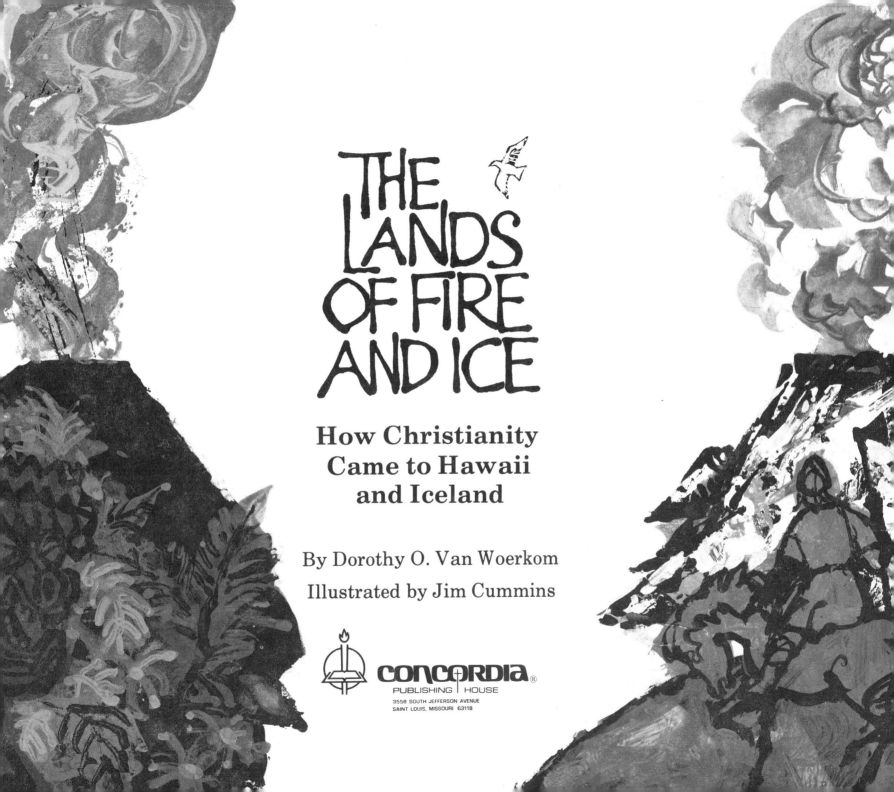

THE LANDS OF FIRE AND ICE

How Christianity Came to Hawaii and Iceland

By Dorothy O. Van Woerkom

Illustrated by Jim Cummins

CONCORDIA ®
PUBLISHING HOUSE
3558 SOUTH JEFFERSON AVENUE
SAINT LOUIS, MISSOURI 63118

Library of Congress Catalog Card Number:
ISBN 0-570-03472-8

Printed in the United States of America

Library of Congress Cataloging in Publication Data

Van Woerkom, Dorothy.
        The lands of fire and ice.

        SUMMARY: Two stories relate how Christianity came to be accepted by the people of Hawaii and Iceland.
        1. Missions—Hawaii—Juvenile literature.
2. Kapiolani, d. 1841—Juvenile literature.
3. Missions—Iceland—Juvenile literature.
[1. Missions—Hawaii. 2. Missions—Iceland]
I. Title.
BV2803.H3V36   266'.009491'2   79-11093
ISBN 0-570-03472-8

For Norma Jean Durrett and the
students at St. Francis de Sales

Bending Arch of Heaven

Preface

The volcano of Kilauea on the Island of Hawaii is the largest active crater in the world. One of its most violent eruptions occurred just thirty years before the opening events of this story—within the memory of many who would be involved in what was about to take place.

For many centuries, the Hawaiian people had believed that Kilauea was the home of the goddess Pele, whose power to destroy them filled them with awe and fear.

The worship of Pele was part of everyday life in the islands when, on April 4, 1820, missionaries from the American Board of Missionaries in Boston arrived. They landed in the District governed by Kapiolani and her husband Naihe—both high chiefs of noble blood and very popular among the islanders.

Kapiolani and Naihe were among the first to accept the teachings of these missionaries. Eventually others of the nobility were converted, but four years of missionary effort failed to break Pele's spell over most of the other people.

In December 1824, Kapiolani set out to break Pele's hold on the people. She had to overcome objections from her husband and her friends, who still feared the ancient goddess. She made the journey from her home to the volcano—a distance of about 150 miles—mostly on foot, determined to defy the wrath of Pele. This, Kapiolani thought, was the only way to prove that Pele did not exist.

Historians of her time called this defiance "one of the greatest acts of moral courage ever performed." Through it, Kapiolani broke the strong bonds of pagan superstition and led her people to the gradual acceptance of Christianity.

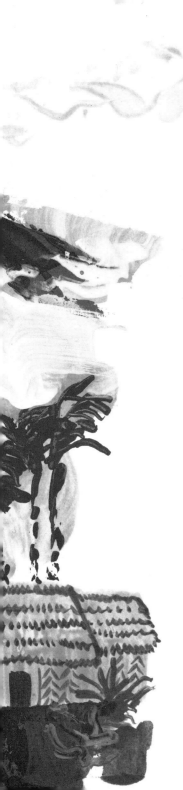

Bending
Arch of Heaven

The True Story of Hawaii

In Hawaii, long ago, Ka-pi-o-la-ni lived. In the language of the islands, her name meant *Bending Arch of Heaven*. She was a brave young leader of her people, and when she spoke they listened.

One day, Bending Arch of Heaven was sitting on a rock among the palm trees, bathing with the sweet oil of a coconut. She heard the voice of Na-i-he, *the Spear,* who was her husband.

"Ka-pi-o-la-ni!" he was shouting. "Look—a ship is coming!"

Bending Arch of Heaven slid down from her rock. The Spear was splashing through the water. Others hurried from their small grass huts and ran to meet the ship.

Four strange men came ashore. Their skin was pale. Their clothes were dark and rough. The Spear and Bending Arch of Heaven spoke to them in welcome.

"We have come from Boston, in America," the strangers said, "to tell you all about the God of Christians."

But the people of Hawaii did not want to listen. They already had a god. Her name was Pe-le. Her home was in the pit of fire on the mountain.

When the people pleased her, Pe-le kept her fire down inside this pit. Only clouds of steam and smoke, and sometimes streaks of redness in the sky, reminded them that she was there.

7

But when the people made her angry, Pe-le roared and made the mountain tremble. Then out would pour her fire, melting rocks and sending hot black rivers flowing down the mountain. And all would have to leave their homes in fear and haste.

There were berry bushes growing on this mountain. These were Pe-le's berries. No one dared to eat them, unless they first threw some to Pe-le in her fire pit. Every day the people did this. Every day they prayed to Pe-le.

"Pe-le is our god," the people told the pale-skinned men. "We do not need the God of Christians."

But Bending Arch of Heaven listened as the strangers spoke of God, who made the world and all things in it.

"Even Pe-le?" Bending Arch of Heaven asked.

"Even Pe-le's fire?" asked the Spear.

A man called Joseph answered. "God made that mountain, and the fire in it. But there is no Pe-le living there. She is something someone made up, long ago. There are no gods who live in mountains. There is just one God—the God who MADE those mountains."

"Tell us more," begged Bending Arch of Heaven.

Joseph smiled and said, "Come back tomorrow, and I will."

So every day the Spear and Bending Arch of Heaven came to hear what Joseph had to say. One day they brought some friends. Then more friends came.

Then one day Bending Arch of Heaven said, "I believe what Joseph tells us. God is God, and Jesus is His Son. And there IS no god named Pe-le!"

9

"I believe it, too," her husband said. And many of their friends agreed.

But the mountain smoked and steamed. The sky grew red. The people cried, "Ka-pi-o-la-ni, you will anger Pe-le! She will send her fires down to punish us!" And after that, when Bending Arch of Heaven spoke they held their ears.

She tried to find a way to make them listen.

"I know!" she said. "I will climb down into Pe-le's pit. When they see that God protects me from the fire, they will believe in Him and not in Pe-le!"

The Spear was very frightened. "I believe in Joseph's God," he said. "But I still believe in Pe-le—just a little."

Bending Arch of Heaven said, "Oh, Na-i-he, there IS no Pe-le." And she told the people what she planned to do.

The next day she began the long walk to the mountain.

"Please do not go," her husband begged.

"I must," she said. "It is the only way."

The Spear said, "Then I am going, too."

Her friends went also. They were afraid, but they would not let her go without them.

"Why don't we sing?" said Bending Arch of Heaven. "We can sing a hymn to God who made this mountain."

They walked and sang, and people came to watch and listen.

11

For miles and miles they walked. They walked for days and days. Then up and up they climbed. Darkness had come when they reached the pit. Great tongues of fire leaped high into the sky. Sparks flew about like flaming, falling stars. The thundering noises hurt their ears. The warm ground shook beneath their feet.

"Pe-le! It is Pe-le!" someone screamed. And many ran back down the mountain.

"Wait!" called Bending Arch of Heaven. "God will not let the fire harm us, you will see."

She looked around. There was Joseph coming toward her, tall and dark against the fire's glow. She smiled at him and raised her hand for silence.

"Listen to what I tell you," she shouted. Her voice was clear and loud above the roar inside the pit. Those who had been talking now were quiet. Those who were running away turned back.

"Tomorrow I go down to Pe-le's pit," she told them. "If I die, then you may all believe in Pe-le. But if I live, then you will know that my God is the only God!"

"You will die, Ka-pi-o-la-ni!" someone said. And she could hear loud weeping all around her.

When morning came, Bending Arch of Heaven walked to the rim of the pit and looked down.

"There," she said pointing. "We will climb down onto that ledge."

13

The ledge was far below the rim of the pit, and very near to the thundering fountains of fire. She picked a large cluster of Pe-le's berries and began the long, dangerous descent.

She turned back to look at her husband. "Will you come, Na-i-he?" she asked.

The Spear looked very worried, but he nodded his head and stepped into the pit. Many of their friends also went on the long, steep hike down to the black ledge far below.

The ledge was hot. It burned their feet as they stood and watched the boiling lake of melted rock rimmed all around by fire. Tall fingers of flame hissed and crackled at them, nearly touching them.

Bending Arch of Heaven picked up a stone. She threw it far out into the black lake. Then she held up the cluster of berries.

"Are you there, Pe-le?" she cried. "I do not think so! Only God is here, protecting us." And she began to eat the berries.

In silence, they all waited on the ledge. Was Pe-le near them, watching? Or was God beside them in the pit, protecting them? They prayed to God and waited. Bending Arch of Heaven threw another stone.

The fire roared and crackled. Gray clouds of steam floated all around them in a heavy mist that made it difficult to breathe. Below them churned the melted rock in mighty waves.

But that was all. No Pe-le came to push them off the ledge. No Pe-le came to scorch them with her fire.

The Spear began to sing a hymn. The others joined him, softly at the start, and then their voices rose and filled the fire pit. Singing with them, Bending Arch of Heaven led the long climb back.

When they reached the top, all could see that none of them were harmed.

"There is no Pe-le!" someone shouted. "Ka-pi-o-la-ni and her God have shown us this!"

The people on the mountain cheered. Runners raced from town to town to spread the news.

And once again, when Bending Arch of Heaven spoke, her people listened.

Ice and Fire

Preface

Iceland was one of the first civilized countries in the world where the people ruled themselves. In the year A.D. 930 they established the world's first Parliament, which they called the Althing. In the Icelandic language "thing" means "a place to talk things over."

Every year for three weeeks in June, the people's representatives, called chieftains, met at the Althing to make the laws and to settle arguments among the people. They held trials by jury, just as democratic countries do today.

In those times, many Icelanders worshiped the gods Odin and Thor, while others were Christians. Then, in the year 1000, the chieftains met to decide whether Iceland should adopt the Christian faith.

While this meeting was taking place, a volcano began erupting not far from the farmstead of Thorodd, one of the chieftains. Some of the people saw this as a sign that Odin would punish them because they had considered accepting Christianity as their national religion.

Snorre, a Christian chieftain, stepped forward boldly and proved to everyone that Odin had no power over them.

What took place that day at the Althing in A.D. 1000 is the true story of how Iceland became a Christian country.

Ice and Fire

The True Story of Iceland

Iceland is a land with fields of snow, and mountains filled with fire. There are pools where water bubbles, hot and steamy. There are miles and miles of ice that never melts.

Long ago these people worshiped gods who lived only in stories. Odin, they said, was the leader of the gods. Then some Christian families came to Iceland. They tried to tell the others all about the one true God.

Snorre was a boy who lived in a Christian family. His closest friend was Thorodd. The two did everything together. They liked to walk along the same trails and play the same games. The only time they ever disagreed was when they talked about God and Odin.

"Odin is the true god," Thorodd said.

"No," said Snorre. "Jesus is."

Snorre and Thorodd often played at being chieftains. These were important men chosen by the people to make the laws and settle arguments. They wore bands of heavy silver on their arms, just above the elbow. When people had to take an oath to tell the truth, they would touch their chieftain's armband and swear that what they said was absolutely true. When Snorre and Thorodd played this game, they wore armbands carved from whalebone.

One day Thorodd put his hand on Snorre's armband. "I promise always to be your friend, no matter what might come between us when we are men," he said.

Then Snorre put his hand on Thorodd's armband. "I will be your friend, too, no matter what. I promise."

They were playing in the place where all the chieftains met each summer. This was a great black hollow on a mountainside. It was horseshoe-shaped, with black cliffs rising high on three sides and a wide black valley of rock spreading out in front. Many, many years before, the mountain had exploded from a fire burning deep inside. It spewed out tons of melted rock called lava. The lava tore the mountain open and slid slowly out across the valley. When the lava cooled, it turned to hard black rock again.

Now the chieftains used this hollow for their meetings, and the people gathered in the valley to listen to them speak.

Thorodd jumped up onto a large piece of lava rock facing the hollow. "I am the speaker today," he shouted. "I am standing here on the Law Rock, telling all the people about the laws of Iceland!"

"You will make a fine chieftain someday," Snorre told him. "So will I. We will always do the right thing. We will make Iceland the greatest country in all the world!"

A noisy raven flew down and landed on a nearby rock. It began to strut back and forth, croaking loudly. It cocked its head and looked at Thorodd with bright black eyes.

Snorre laughed. "You had better get down from there," he said. "Chieftain Smart-feathers wants to be the speaker now."

23

Thorodd jumped down from the rock. "I will race you home," he said.

Snorre raced him to a little house made from slabs of lava rock, all covered over with growing grass. He touched the grass on the low rock fence in front of the house. "I win this time!" he said, and he kept on running until he reached his own house farther down the road.

For many years Snorre and Thorodd kept their promise. In all of Iceland there were no more loyal friends than they. And just as they had pretended long before, they did become great chieftains. How proud they were, and happy to be working for their country.

But more and more people in Iceland were turning away from the old gods and becoming Christians. This made Snorre glad, but Thorodd did not like it at all.

"Why are the people doing this?" he would say. "Everyone knows that Odin is the true god."

"Not everyone," Snorre said.

Then the people began to quarrel about God and Odin. Sons quarreled with their fathers. Wives quarreled with their husbands. Friends quarreled with each other.

One day Snorre and Thorodd were standing in a bright green meadow on Thorodd's farm, watching lambs playing with their mothers. High above them the snow-covered mountaintops were golden in the sunlight.

"We must do something about all this quarreling," Snorre said. "Our country will soon be at war over it. Surely one religion is enough for Iceland! We must ask everyone to become a Christian so there will be peace again."

"You are right that there should be only one religion in Iceland," Thorodd said. "But it should be the old one of the god Odin!"

Snorre looked up at the sun. "In a little while it will be time for our midsummer meeting. I am going to tell the people that we must all vote to become Christians."

"Then you are no longer any friend of mine!" Thorodd said. His voice shook with with fury and his eyes looked angrily into Snorre's. "I will tell the people to keep the old religion. If it was good enough for our fathers and our grandfathers, it is good enough for us and for our children."

After that day, neither Snorre nor Thorodd would speak to each other. When they passed on the road, they would put their horses to a gallop, looking down at the ground or up at the mountains.

People noticed this and were saddened by it, but it still did not stop them from fighting among themselves.

At last, in the cool, fresh-smelling days of midsummer, the chieftains came from the nearby villages and from far away farms for their meeting. Their families and servants and many of their friends came with them. They put up little huts in the valley where they could sleep at night.

On the first day of the meeting, hundreds of people were gathered in the valley. Soon the bell ringers were ringing out the signal that the meeting was about to start. The chieftains walked briskly to their places in the hollow, and Speaker Olaf stepped up onto the Law Rock. The sunlight flashed along his silver armband as he raised his arm for silence. Then Speaker Olaf began to recite all the laws of Iceland for the people to hear.

"Now," said Olaf when he had finished, "we are ready to decide on this question of religion. Will we keep the god Odin, or will we honor the God of the Christians? Those who wish to speak, come forward."

Some of the chieftains came up to the Law Rock to tell why they would vote for Odin. Others spoke of Jesus and His miracles.

For three days the chieftains talked and the people listened. On the third day a horse's hooves rang loudly against the rocky floor of the quiet valley. A horseman rode full speed toward the meeting place. People made way for him as he dismounted and ran through the crowd. He hurried straight to the Law Rock and spoke to Olaf. People began whispering to each other. What was happening?

Speaker Olaf raised his arm for silence. "The mountain Aulfus is throwing out fire! Hot lava is pouring down its sides."

"Aulfus is near my farm!" Thorodd shouted. "See what comes of all this talk about Christianity? Now Odin is angry with us. He has stirred up the mountain's fire to destroy us!"

The chieftains and the people all began talking at once. "Odin is angry!" they said. "We will be destroyed!"

Some were on their knees praying aloud for Jesus to save them.

Snorre rushed over to the Law Rock and jumped up beside Olaf. Again Olaf raised his arm. No one noticed. He signaled for the bell ringers to ring their bells.

"Listen!" Olaf shouted when there was quiet once more. "Chieftain Snorre has something to say."

Snorre looked down at the other chieftains. He looked around at the people.

"Think of where we are today," he said. "Think of where we are standing. Our meeting place was formed when this mountain exploded with fire and sent hot lava pouring down. It all happened long ago, before our time and before the time of our grandfathers. There was no talk then of becoming Christians, so why did the mountain send out its fire? What was there to punish people for then?"

Thorodd was staring up at Snorre. He looked angry. Then he looked surprised. Then he looked puzzled. At last he smiled at Snorre and his lips began moving.

"Have you something to say, Chieftain Thorodd?" Speaker Olaf asked.

Thorodd climbed onto the Law Rock and threw his arm around Snorre's shoulders. "Chieftain Snorre speaks wisely," he said. "Many of our mountains roar with fire. We all know that! This is a danger that we live with every day. But what have those fires to do with what we speak of here at our meeting? Nothing! Now, what do you say? I, for one, will cast my vote for Christianity!"

"So say I!" one of the chieftains shouted.

"And I!"

"And I!"

So that was how Iceland became a land of Christians. The people were quite happy with their choice, but happiest of all was Thorodd. The flowing lava stopped before it reached his farm. His lambs were safe. And he was friends again with Snorre!

31

Bibliography

Alexander, W. D. *A Brief History of the Hawaiian People*. New York: American Book Company, 1891.

Ellis, William. *Journal of William Ellis, A Narrative of a Tour Through Hawaii in 1823*. Honolulu: Hawaiian Gazette Co., Ltd., 1917 (reprint of the London 1827 edition).

Golden, Grace Blaisdell. *Made in Iceland*. New York: Alfred A. Knopf, 1959.

Peck, Helen E. *Iceland and Greenland*. New York: Abelard-Schuman, 1966.

Vitaliano, Dorothy B. *Legends of the Earth: Their Geologic Origins*. Bloomington: Indiana University Press, 1973.

Westervelt, W. D. *Hawaiian Legends of Volcanoes*. Boston: Ellis Press, 1916.

Withington, Antionette. *The Golden Cloak*. Hawaii: Hawaiian Press, 1953.

Wyndette, Olive. *Islands of Destiny: A History of Hawaii*. Tokyo: Charles E. Tuttle Co., 1968.